CW00411216

3

49 Excuses for Staying Up Past Your Bedtime

Copyright © 2016, 2022 by James Warwood

Published by Curious Squirrel Press

Book cover design by: James Warwood
Book interior design by: Mala Letra / Lic. Sara F. Salomon

ISBN: 9798433487741
ebook ISBN: B0IEQH6UMO

THE EXCUSE

Book Six:
49 Excuses for Staying Up
Past Your Bedtime

ENCYCLOPEDIA

James Warwood

BOOK SIX

Excuses for Staying Up Past Your Bedtime

BEDTIME EXCUSES

Zzzz

1. THE UNDER THE BED EXCUSE

Mum, I don't want to alarm you but there is something under my bed . . .

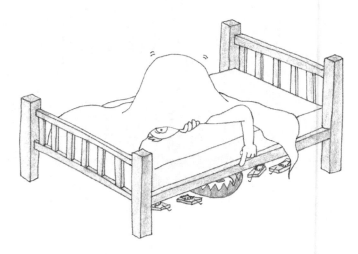

. . . You are not allowed to turn off the light until I am 100% sure there are no monsters hiding under there. Could you check it for me please?

2. THE EVIL TEDDY EXCUSE

I would go to bed, in fact I want to go to bed. It's just . . .

. . . My teddy bear is evil! Ever since we put him in the washing machine after I dropped him in that muddy puddle, Marshmallow has been looking at me funny. It's like he is waiting for me to fall asleep . . . *to exact his revenge.*

3. THE MORNING EXCUSE

What? Go to bed? But it's the morning . . .

. . . The sun has risen and the cockerel has crowed. I had a lovely sleep and I am ready to take on a new day. Can I have a bowl of cereal please?

4. THE INSOMNIA EXCUSE

I've been reading medical journals and doing online research . . .

. . . I have Insomnia: a terrible sleeping disorder which means I can't fall asleep. Honestly, I've tried everything. I just can't fall asleep!

5. THE MEDICAL BREAKTHROUGH EXCUSE

At last my work is complete. Behold the 'Stay-Up-All-Night Pill' . . .

. . . *Gulp* What did you say? Don't swallow the pill. Too late, Dad. Now I've got to stay up all night and make a list of all the side-effects I experience. Is the room spinning or are my eyeballs rolling around on the floor?

6. THE TEMPERATURE EXCUSE

I'M TOO HOT, I NEED TO TAKE MY VEST OFF

NOW I'M TOO COLD, I NEED TO PUT ON THICKER SOCKS

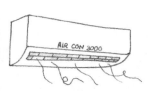

NOW I'M TOO HOT AGAIN, TURN THE AIR CON TO FULL POWER

NOW I'M TOO COLD AGAIN, TURN THE RADIATOR TO FULL POWER

. . . Repeat until you've run out of ideas, then claim to be suffering from sunstroke and hypothermia at the same time.

7. THE NIGHT SCHOOL TRIP EXCUSE

What does it look like I'm doing? I'm packing for the night school trip . . .

. . . Strange, I thought I told you about my class star gazing expedition. Anyway, I can't talk now, I've got lots of packing to do.

8. THE STUCK IN THE BATH EXCUSE

I fell asleep in the bath . . .

. . . Then the temperature dropped below freezing and now I'm frozen solid. I'm stuck in the bath. Now I've got to wait until I completely thaw out before I can go to bed.

9. THE STORYTIME EXCUSE

I do miss the days when you'd read me a bedtime story . . .

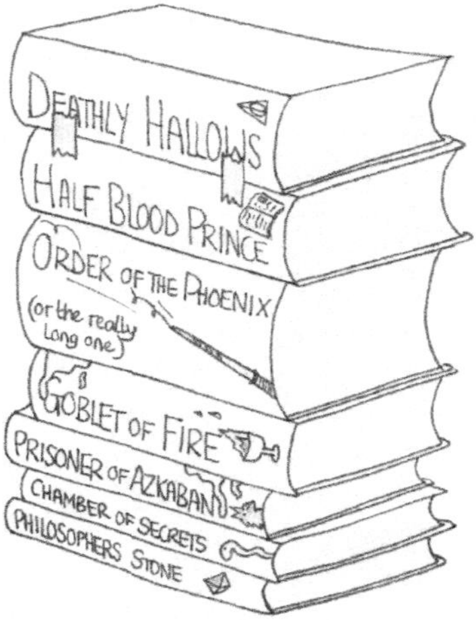
DEATHLY HALLOWS
HALF BLOOD PRINCE
ORDER OF THE PHOENIX
(or the really Long one)
GOBLET OF FIRE
PRISONER OF AZKABAN
CHAMBER OF SECRETS
PHILOSOPHERS STONE

. . . So I decided to glue together all my Harry Potter Books. Now you can read them to me back to back in one sitting. I'm ready when you are.

10. THE MONDAYS EXCUSE

I can't go sleep. It's Sunday night . . .

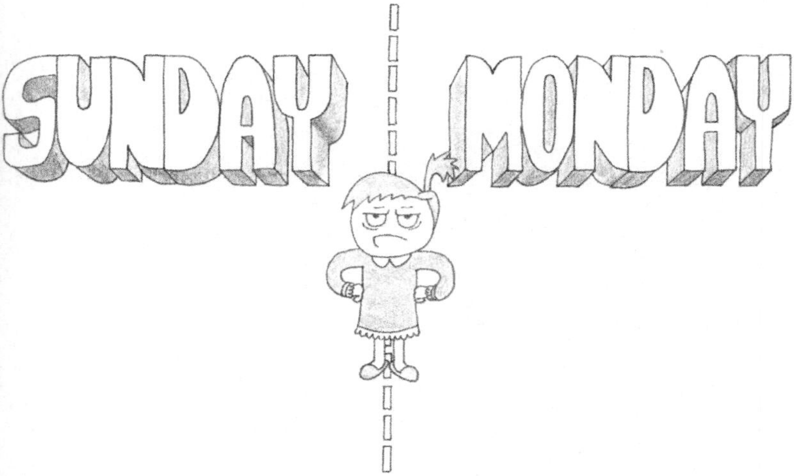
SUNDAY
MONDAY

. . . If we all go to bed then we are allowing Monday - *the worst of all the days* - to creep up and shackle us to another week. But not me, I'm going to live in between the weekend and the week forever and ever. Go on, try and stop me!

11. THE RESTRAINING ORDER EXCUSE

Bad news, my bed has filed a restraining order against me . . .

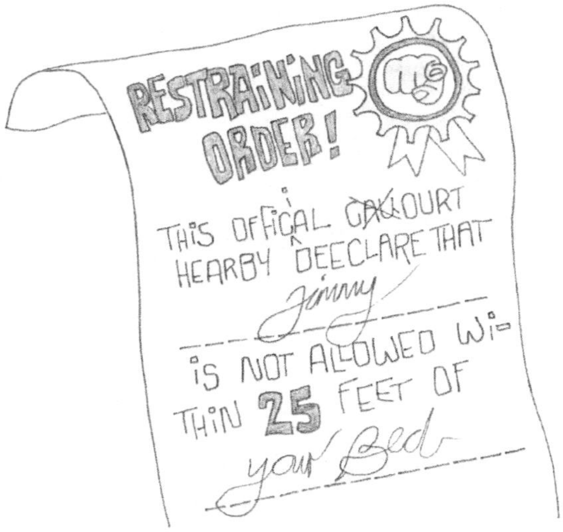
RESTRAINING ORDER!
THIS OFFICAL COURT HEARBY DEECLARE THAT
Jimmy
IS NOT ALLOWED WITHIN 25 FEET OF
your Bed

. . . I can't go within 25 feet of my bed or I'll be thrown in jail. The bed lawyers told me that it felt unappreciated and was tired of being walked all over.

12. THE X-MEN EXCUSE

Finally, I've been accepted. Xaviers School for Gifted Children have recognised my genetic mutation . . .

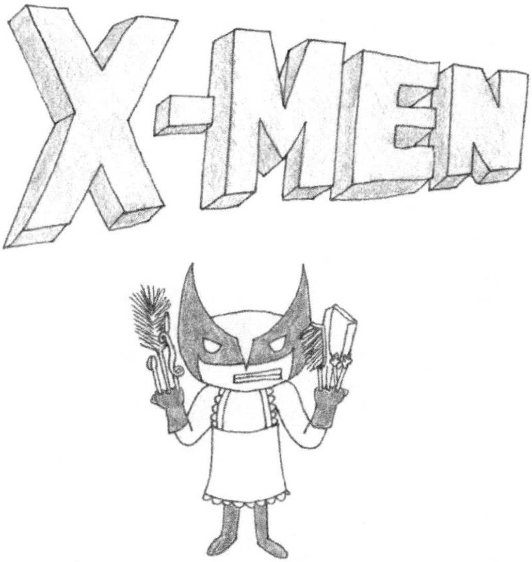
X-MEN

. . . I don't sleep. My brain never needs to rest and my muscles regenerate all by themselves. So I can make the morning brew and do all the cleaning while all the other X-Men are fast asleep.

13. THE HUNGRY SOFA EXCUSE

Help! The sofa is trying to eat me . . .

. . . I've probably got two hours left to live until the sofa has finished slowly digesting me. Goodbye Mum, goodbye Dad. My one dying wish is for you to switch the TV back on and bring me a glass of milk and a cookie.

14. THE WORK EXPERIENCE EXCUSE

Did you get the letter from school explaining my work experience programme starts tonight . . .

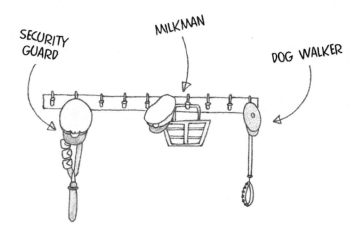

SECURITY GUARD

MILKMAN

DOG WALKER

. . . From 8pm – 2am I'll be a Security Guard, from 2am – 6am I'll be a Milkman, and from 6am – 8am I'll be a Dog Walker. Wish me luck on my first night shift.

15. THE NEGOTIATION EXCUSE

I know that my bedtime is normally 8pm and my older brother goes to bed at 10pm, but . . .

. . . Me and my older brother have had a mature conversation and we've decided that it would be better for both of us if you were to swap our bedtimes.

16. THE GOLDEN MOON EXCUSE

I can't go to bed now, otherwise I'll miss a once-in-a-million years phenomenon . . .

. . . It's called *The Golden Moon*. What does it look like? Well let me stay up all night and we can find out together.

17. THE SELF-TORTURE EXCUSE

I've forgotten where I left my homework . . .

. . . So now I've got to torture the information out of myself. If I were you I'd leave me to it. This could get ugly.

18. THE STUDYING EXCUSE

I have decided to take your advice and read more books . . .

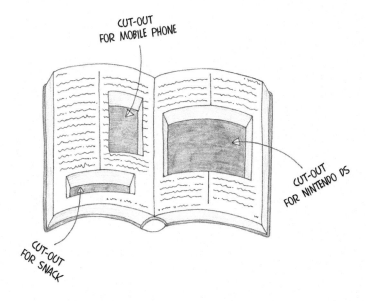

CUT-OUT FOR MOBILE PHONE

CUT-OUT FOR NINTENDO DS

CUT-OUT FOR SNACK

. . . I will of course have to catch up on all the reading and studying I've missed so tonight I am going to stay up all night and read the Bible from cover to cover.

19. THE LIST OF DEMANDS EXCUSE

Of course mama, I'll go to bed like a nice little girl . . .

. . . as soon as you have completed this list of demands!

20. THE MISSING TEDDY EXCUSE

Oh no, Teddy is missing. I can't go to bed without Teddy . . .

. . . I must have left him at Grandma's house. I think Teddy is inside Grandma's unbreakable safe behind the secret door hidden at the bottom of the locked basement. I'll wait in my bedroom until you've found Teddy and brought him back.

21. THE CONCOCTION EXCUSE

There was once a boy called George who had a marvellous idea . . .

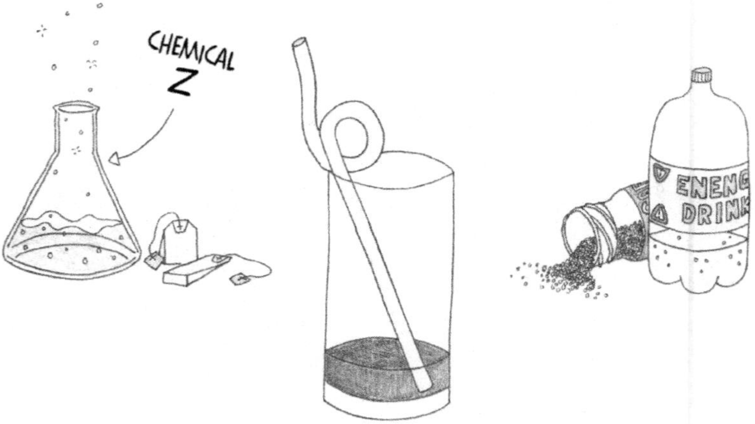
CHEMICAL
Z

. . . He has inspired me to make my very own marvellous medicine to help me stay up all night. If you need me I'll be bouncing from one wall to the next until morning.

22. THE SUPPER EXCUSE

I can't go to bed until I've had my supper . . .

. . . I'd like a three course supper tonight. I'll start with the French Onion Soup with Parmesan Croutons. For main I'll have the Pigeon Breast in Red Wine with Potatoes Au Gratin. And for dessert the Vanilla Crème Brûlée with Goji Berries . . . And don't forget the Tomato Ketchup.

23. THE SELF-HYPNOTISM EXCUSE

I bought this self-hypnotism kit from the internet to help with my bedtime . . .

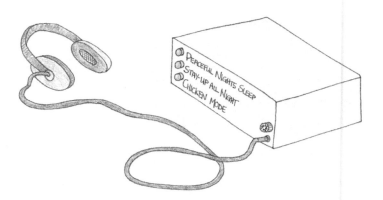

PEACEFUL NIGHTS SLEEP
STAY-UP ALL NIGHT
CHICKEN MODE

. . . The only problem is that the User Manual is missing. It looks very confusing. I do hope I get this right.

24. THE BRAIN FLU EXCUSE

I can't fall asleep. I think I have Brain Flu . . .

. . . What? You haven't heard of Brain Flu? It is a terrible disease of the brain that can turn you into a vegetable and the only cure is to starve your brain of sleep by staying up all night. Oh yeah, and it is highly contagious and transmitted through brain waves.

25. THE PRACTISING EXCUSE

Pardon, did you ask me what I am doing? . . .

. . . I am practising to become a professional ballet dancer, a world-class musician and a plate spinning champion all at the same time. I can't waste my precious time on *sleep*. Trust me, when I'm winning awards and making millions I'll remember how you let me stay up all night to practise and mention you in my acceptance speeches.

26. THE THIRSTY EXCUSE

I'm really thirsty, can I have a drink please? . . .

. . . Oh dear, now I really need a wee, can I go to the toilet? Now I'm thirsty again, can I have a drink please? Now I need a wee again . . . *repeat until your parent looks angry, then suggest they should drink a glass of water to calm down.*

27. THE WET THE BED EXCUSE

Mum, I've got something embarrassing to tell you . . .

. . . I mistook my bedroom for the bathroom and wet the bed. I thought the taps were some sort of new feature to control the heated mattress. Please don't tell any of my friends about this.

28. THE WINSTON CHURCHILL EXCUSE

Did you know that Winston Churchill only had 3 hours of sleep a night while he was planning the D-Day landings . . .

D-DINNER DAY LANDINGS:
BIG DISTRACTION!
ENTRY POINT
PUDDING CUPBOARD

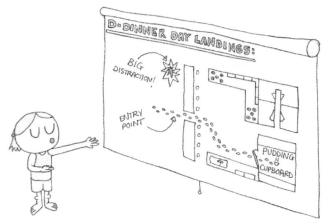

. . . I'm planning something similar. I'm planning the D-D-Day Landings. I am going to infiltrate enemy territory in a covert operation to steal highly classified school secrets. So I will need to stay up all night for the rest of the week to perfect my plans.

29. THE CRICKETS EXCUSE

The crickets outside are very loud, aren't they . . .

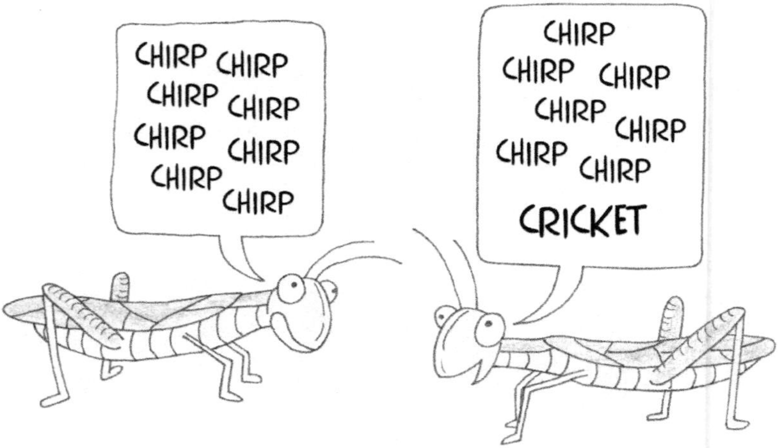
CHIRP CHIRP CHIRP CHIRP CHIRP CHIRP CHIRP CHIRP
CHIRP CHIRP CHIRP CHIRP CHIRP CHIRP CHIRP CRICKET

. . . What are they saying? Why do they talk so loud? When do they go to sleep? How do the birds sleep while the crickets are talking? Where do birds sleep? When do they wake up?

30. THE TOOTH TRAP EXCUSE

What, go to bed? But I need to stay up all night and hold this rope . . .

. . . I am going to do what no child has done before. I am going to catch the Tooth Fairy.

31. THE PHONE CALL EXCUSE

Is that the phone, don't worry I'll get it . . .

. . . Hello this is Jimmy speaking *pause* what, you've captured Scooby Doo, Ash Ketchum and SpongeBob Square Pants *pause* they are dangling over a tank of sharks with laser beams attached their tails *pause* and you're going to cut the rope if I stop playing videos games all night *pause* ok, ok, I'll play video games all night, just don't kill my favourite TV characters!

32. THE CHINA EXCUSE

I know it is 9pm, so it's time for bed . . .

. . . but I've decided I'm Chinese now. It's 9am in China so I better go, I'm late for school.

33. THE BED BUGS EXCUSE

You know how you bought me that microscope for my birthday . . .

. . . I found this mutant Bed Bug in my pillow. I hope you agree I can't share a bed with that thing, it clearly snores and will probably steal the duvet!

34. THE COUNTING SHEEP EXCUSE

Tonight I'd like to try a new idea to help me fall asleep . . .

. . . Apparently counting sheep helps you sleep so I've built a fence and designed these sheep costumes. If you and Dad and Grandma and Grandpa and my older brother could wear them and jump over this fence I would be very grateful.

35. THE EYELIDS EXCUSE

I don't want to go to sleep . . .

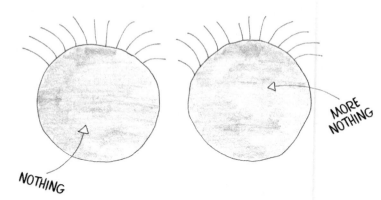

NOTHING

MORE NOTHING

. . . The insides of my eyelids are soooooooooooooooooooooooooooooooooo boring to look at!

36. THE UNCOMFORTABLE EXCUSE

I can't go to sleep. My bed is really uncomfortable . . .

. . . Don't panic, I've taken care of it. Would anyone like a marshmallow on a stick? Oh, and I need a new bed.

37. THE KISS GOODNIGHT EXCUSE

I forgot to give you a goodnight kiss and while I am downstairs I might as well say goodnight to everyone I love . . .

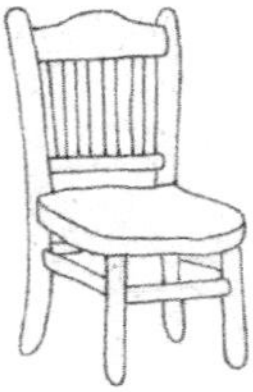

GOODNIGHT KITCHEN CHAIR

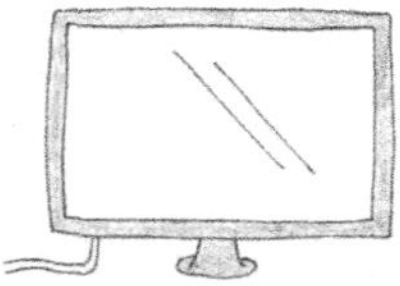

GOODNIGHT TV

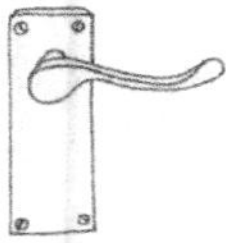

GOODNIGHT DOOR HANDLE

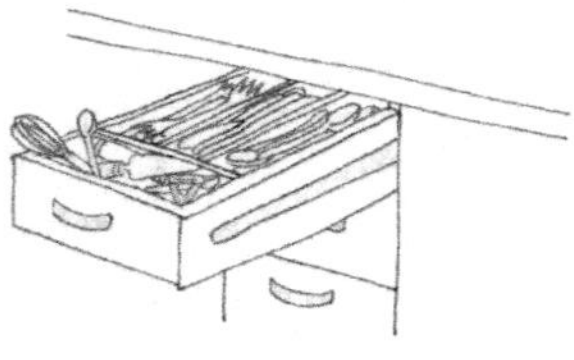

GOODNIGHT KNIVES, FORKS & SPOONS

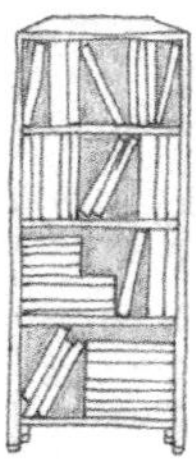

GOODNIGHT BOOKS

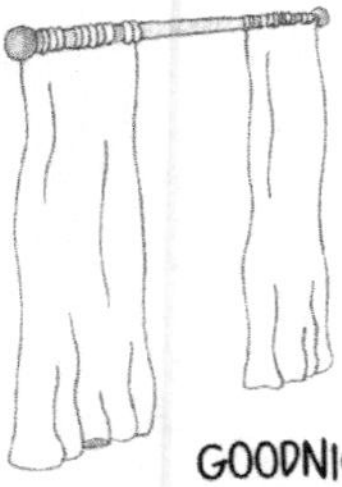

GOODNIGHT CURTAINS

. . . here are some ideas for items you can kiss goodnight. Remember, the possibilities are endless, but I would recommend staying away from the toilet.

38. THE SUNRISE EXCUSE

Science *thinks* it knows everything, but I've made a ground-breaking discovery! . . .

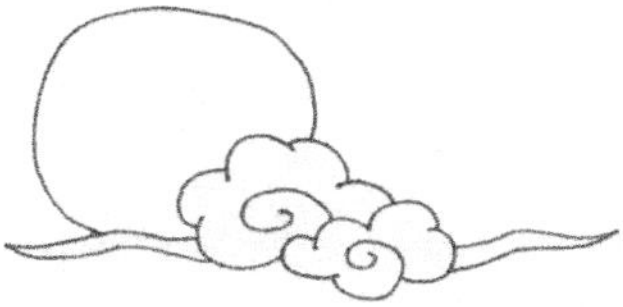

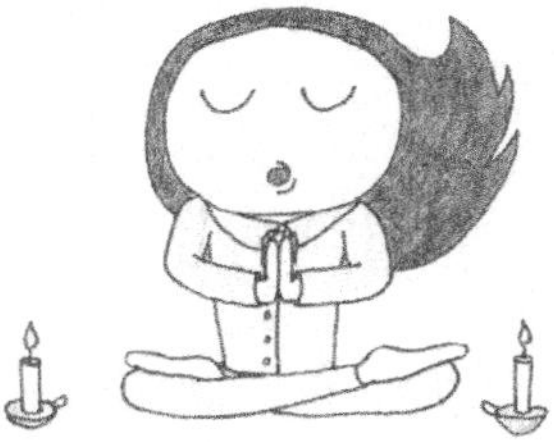

. . . The Sun does not rise every morning because the Earth is orbiting the Sun whilst spinning at 1,041mph. It will only rise if I stay up all night praying to the Moon Goddess so she releases her pet galactic space beetle which pushes the Sun over the horizon and across the sky.

39. THE WHALE EXCUSE

I've been reading on the internet that Whale Song is a relaxing and soothing way to drop off to sleep . . .

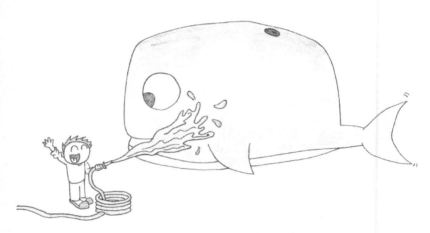

. . . What the Internet does not mention is that you have to hose them down every 15 minutes, feed them plankton every 30 minutes and that Whales are extremely loud and take up a lot of room. But you have to admit, Freckles is really cute, isn't she?

40. THE FLY EXCUSE

I can't sleep because a fly is buzzing around my room . . .

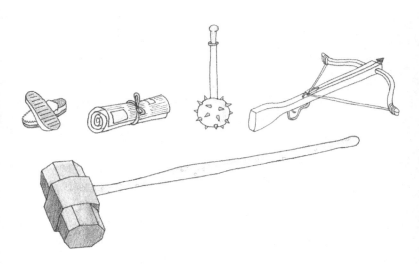

. . . you are going to have to kill it for me. That's right, if you want me to go to bed you will have to become a fly murderer. Choose your weapon wisely.

41. THE ENTREPRENEUR EXCUSE

Mum, Dad, I am now a successful entrepreneur . . .

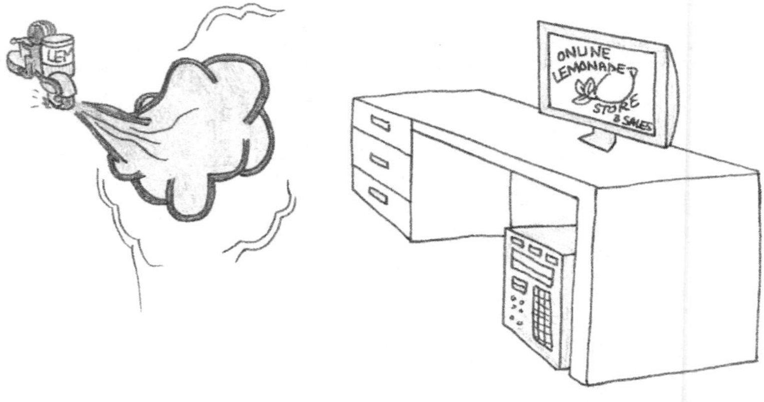
LEM
ONLINE
LEMONADE
STORE
& SALES

. . . This is my business - *The Online Lemonade Stand*. I sell homemade lemonade online. Now if you'll excuse me I've got deliveries to make to Mr. Perkins in London, Mrs. Xing in Shanghai and then I am going to climb to the top of Everest to open the very first mountain-top lemonade stand. Wish me luck.

42. THE SPEECH EXCUSE

Before I go to bed I need to tell you something . . .

. . . I decided to write it all down on these cue cards so that I didn't forget anything. Hope you are sitting comfortably.

43. THE BAKING EXCUSE

Don't disturb me, I'm in the middle of baking you a delicious cake . . .

. . . The next step in the recipe book says to put the cake in the oven for 97 minutes, which just so happens to be the exact running time for my new DVD. You go put the film on and I'll go get the popcorn.

44. THE NOISE EXCUSE

Ok, time for bed. Good ni . . . wait, did you hear a noise . . .

. . . It sounded like there is something outside? You'd better go investigate . . . Then follow your parent down the stairs, lock the door behind them and get comfortable on the sofa in front of the TV.

45. THE MONSTERS EXCUSE

I'm scared! Please check my bedroom for monsters before I go to bed . . . But before you go in there, these are the monsters you are looking for:

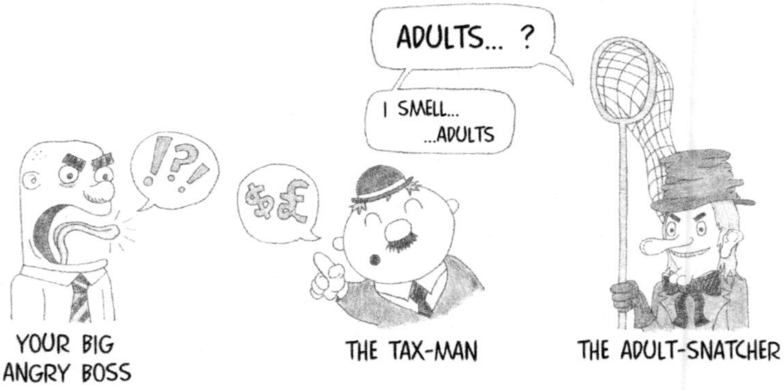
ADULTS... ?
I SMELL...
...ADULTS
!?!
$£
YOUR BIG
ANGRY BOSS
THE TAX-MAN
THE ADULT-SNATCHER

1. Your Big Angry Boss (who yells at you for no reason).
2. The Tax-Man (he's been looking for you, something about *overdue taxes.*
3. The Adult-Snatcher (snatches fully grown humans and locks them in his dungeon).

Don't worry if you're as scared as I am. Maybe we could stay up all night together?

46. THE NOCTURNAL EXCUSE

Go to sleep, now? But I've just woken up . . .

. . . Did I forget to tell you I am *nocturnal* now? It means that I go to bed in the daytime and stay awake at night. My bedtime is now 8am, not 8pm. I had a relaxing day's sleep at school and now it's time to get all my jobs done.

47. THE FRIDGE BED EXCUSE

My bed is extremely uncomfortable. I always wake up with backache . . .

. . . So I decided I would give the fridge a try. I had to make room for my pillow and all my teddies. I hope you don't mind.

48. THE NIGHTMARE EXCUSE

But I can't go to sleep, Dad. If I do then the big, nasty crocodile will eat me . . .

. . . I have the same terrifying nightmare every night. Perhaps if you made me a peanut butter sandwich I could give it to the crocodile and we'll become friends.

49. THE UP-SALE EXCUSE

I know that my bedtime time is normally 9pm, but . . .

. . . if I do all my homework on time, tidy my bedroom, wash the car at the weekend and only read my books after 9pm could I stay up till 10pm tonight?

Smile sweetly, enlarge your eyeballs, and don't forget to say please!

BONUS: ALLERGIC EXCUSE

I definitely need to go have a lie down . . .

. . . Why? This might seem like I am overreacting, but I think I am having an allergic reaction to you telling me to 'tidy my bedroom'. I better go and lie on the sofa for the next four hours and watch cartoons.

BONUS: FACEBOOK FRIEND EXCUSE

Dad. I've a deal to make with you . . .

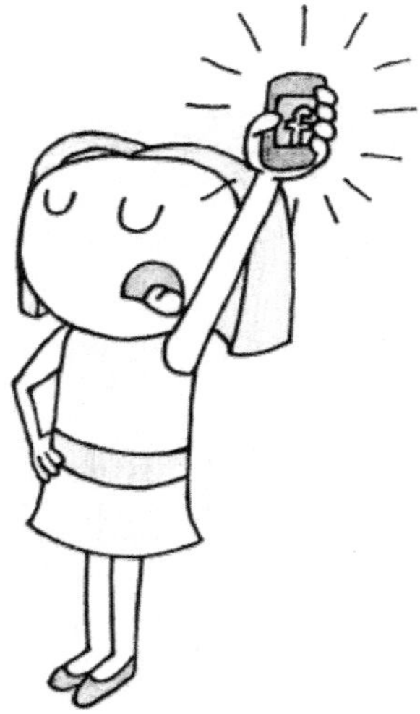
f

. . . If you tidy my bedroom and tell Mum that I did it, I'll one day do you the honour and privilege of adding you as my Facebook friend.

BONUS: READ ALL NIGHT EXCUSE

I love going to bed on time. Night, night . . .

. . . By the way, we need more AA batteries for my torch and I'll need to go to the library tomorrow morning.

BONUS: SHOOTING STAR EXCUSE

My science teacher told us we have to stay up really late tonight . . .

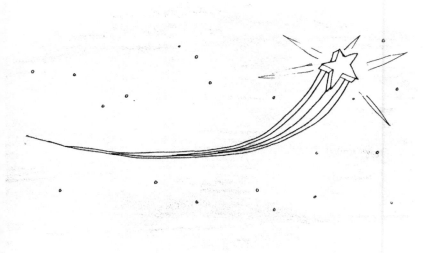

. . . Why? Because if you let me stay up past my bedtime tonight we could see shooting stars. And if we do see any I promise I'll make an unselfish wish.

BONUS: AIRING CUPBOARD EXCUSE

Bad news. Someone has stolen my duvet . . .

. . . And not just mine. Every single duvet in the house has disappeared so no one will be able to go to bed! Don't bother checking the airing cupboard, I've already checked there.

BONUS: HOT COCOA EXCUSE

I CANNOT go to sleep until I've had hot cocoa . . .

. . . Remember, it has to have mini-marshmallows, hand whipped cream and chocolate shavings (all made by a professional French Chocolatier).

BONUS: EVIL FART EXCUSE

I can't go to bed . . .

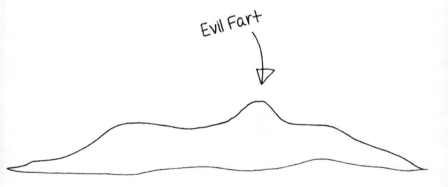

Evil Fart

. . . My older brother has left an evil fart under my duvet (and it's waiting for me).

BONUS: THE MYSTERY SCREW EXCUSE

I'm sure it's nothing, and I'm just being paranoid but . . .

. . . I found this extremely important looking screw under my bed. And it does feel a little on the wobbly side. Maybe I should sleep on the sofa, just for tonight.

BONUS: THE PILLOW OF DOOM EXCUSE

I'm terrified of my pillow . . .

. . . Don't laugh. It's a real fear. If I go to sleep it will rise up and destroy all civilisation. Don't worry, though, as I'm going to stay up and stand guard.

BONUS: NEVER, EVER SLEEP EXCUSE

The Bogeyman, the Grinch, and the Wicked Witch of the West . . .

. . . None of them sleep. And so, therefore, neither do I.

BONUS: TOO HOT EXCUSE

Seriously, it's way too HOT to go to sleep tonight . . .

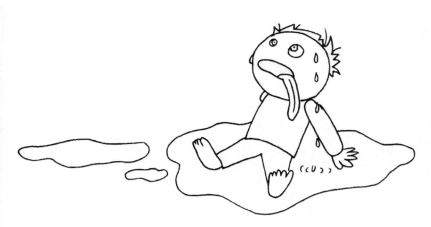

. . . In fact, it's too hot to do anything (except eat ice cream).

BONUS: FACEBOOK THREAT EXCUSE

If you let me stay up late tonight . . .

. . . I promise I will never tell anyone that your life is not as awesome as you pretend it is on Facebook.

BONUS: TOO COLD EXCUSE

Seriously, it's way too cold to go to sleep . . .

. . . I need twenty hot water bottles, a hug from a friendly yeti and a massive mug of hot chocolate before I can go to bed.

ABOUT THE AUTHOR

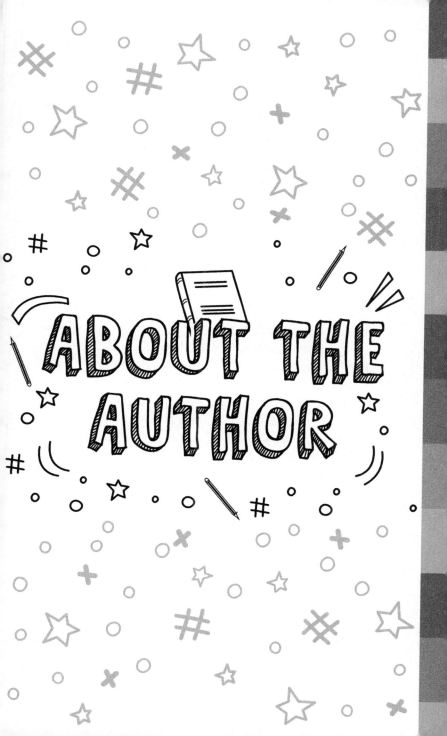

James Warwood is (usually) very good at writing about himself. So he would like to start by saying that this bio was written on an off day.

He lives on the Welsh Border with his wife, two boys, and carnivorous plant. For some unknown reason he chose a career in Customer Service, mainly because it was indoor work and involves no manual labour. He writes and illustrates children's books by night like a superhero.

Anyway, people don't really read these bios, do they? They want to get on with reading a brand new book or play outside, not wade through paragraphs of text that attempts to make the author sound like a really interesting and accomplished person. Erm . . . drat, I've lost my rhythm.

WHERE TO FIND JAMES ONLINE

Website: www.cjwarwood.com
Goodreads: James Warwood
Instagram: CJWarwood
Twitter: @cjwarwood
Facebook: James Warwood

SO, WHAT'S NEXT?

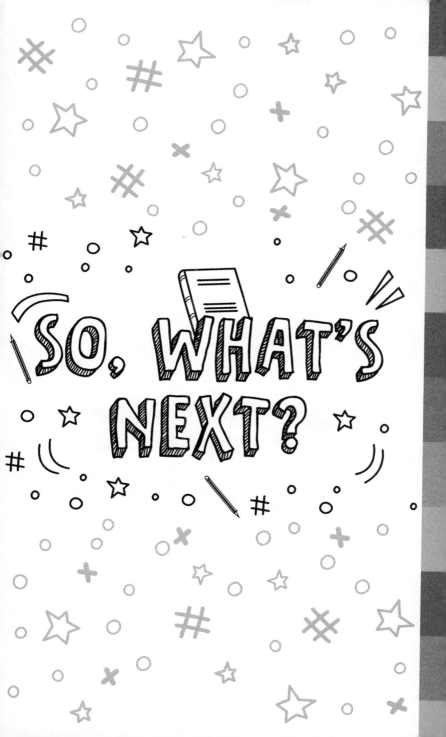

CATASTROPHE
ONE MILLION SOCKS
VANQUISHED
DRAGON

MIDDLE-GRADE STAND-ALONE FICTION

The Chef Who Cooked Up a Catastrophe
The Boy Who Stole One Million Socks
The Girl Who Vanquished the Dragon

TRUTH or POOP?
TRUTH or POOP?
TRUTH or POOP?

TRUTH OR POOP?

True or false quiz books. Learn something new and laugh as you do it!

Book One: Amazing Animal Facts
Book Two: Spectacular Space Facts
Book Three: Gloriously Gross Facts

THE EXCUSE ENCYCLOPEDIA

Eleven more books to read!

Book 1 - 49 Excuses for Not Tidying Your Bedroom
Book 2 - 49 Ways to Steal the Cookie Jar
Book 3 - 49 Excuses for Not Doing Your Homework
Book 4 - 49 Questions to Annoy Your Parents
Book 5 - 49 Excuses for Skipping Gym Class
Book 6 - 49 Excuses for Staying Up Past Your Bedtime
Book 7 - 49 Excuses for Being Really Late
Book 8 - 49 Excuses For Not Eating Your Vegetables
Book 9 - 49 Excuses for Not Doing Your Chores
Book 10 - 49 Excuses for Getting the Most Out of
       Christmas
Book 11 - 49 Excuses for Extending Your Summer
       Holidays
Book 12 - 49 Excuses for Baggin More Candy at
       Halloween

Or get all 12 titles in 1 MASSIVE book!

The Excuse Encyclopedia: Books 1 - 12

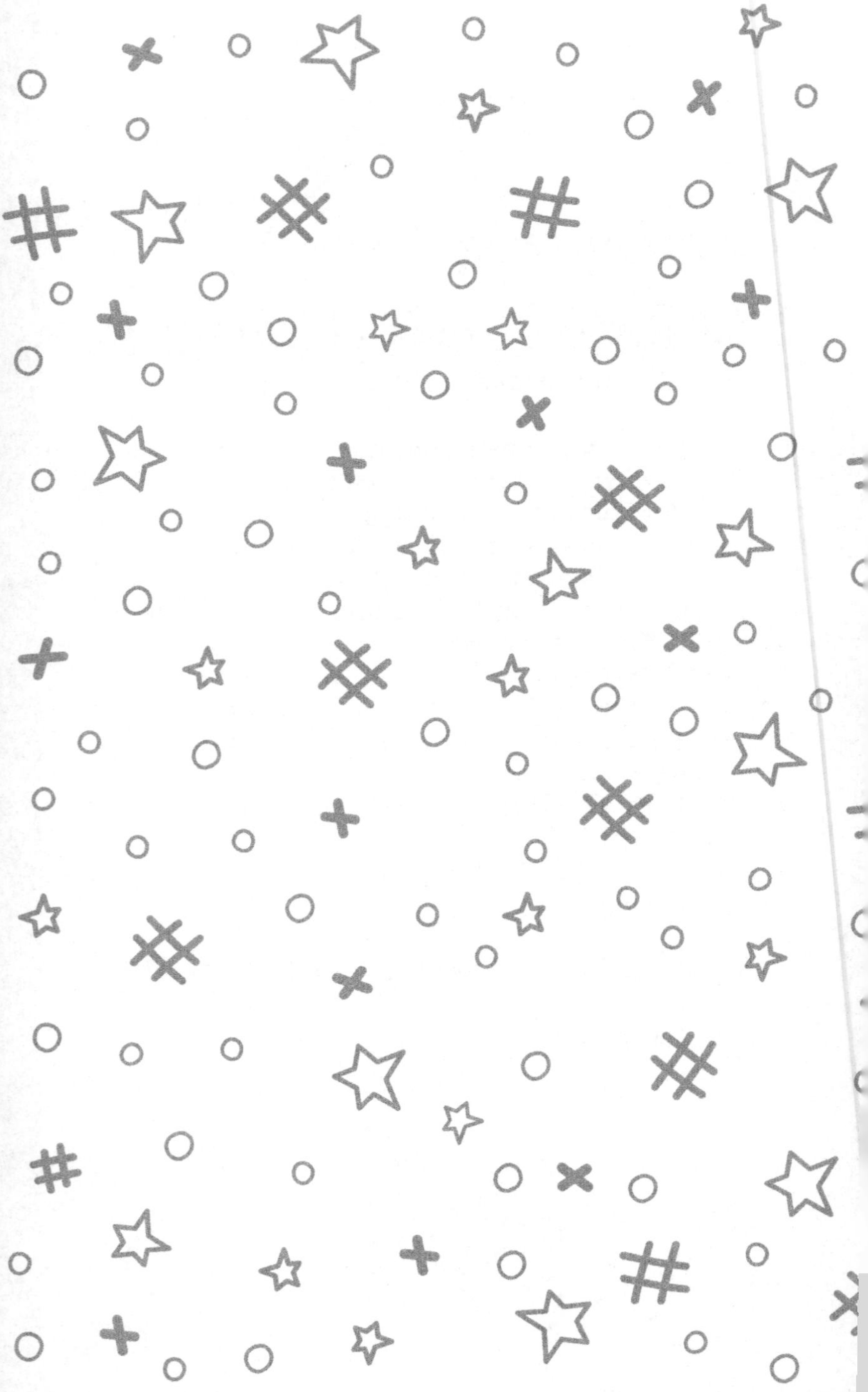

Printed in Great Britain
by Amazon